Lilies of the Valley

LaAsia J. Medlock

Copyright © 2019 by LaAsia J. Medlock

Lilies of the Valley
by LaAsia J. Medlock

Printed in the United States of America

ISBN: 978-1-7336986-7-2

All rights reserved. No part of this document may be reproduced or transmitted in any form, by any means (electronic, photocopying, recording, or otherwise) without the written permission of the author.

READY Media LLC Publishers
Gail Dudley, Publishing Consultant

Cover: Art by LaAsia Medlock
Cover Design: Dominiq Dudley

Introduction

This array of poems is dedicated to the beautiful creation of humanity in the Bride of Christ and those being invited in. These poems were birthed from my secret place with Abba but are mainly inspired by the Holy Bible, the Scriptures breathed from God through Jesus Christ, the Word made manifest; and of the Holy Spirit, the Word manifest in us. The Bible Scriptures will forever be God's poetic heart cry of His endless love for the nations of the world. His love for you is from the inside out, outside in, from bottom up, top down.

You have permission to soak in these poems at times when evil tries to tell you, you are not enough. Do not listen to that voice because the devil is not telling the truth. Listen to the One who is the Truth, the Way, and the Life. His name is Jesus. He is your Light in the Darkness. Your inheritance is life and peace, for you are in His marvelous Light bought with a price of Jesus's Blood and Body. He was broken and bled just for you. And the best part about it is, He is alive forever and ever, and if you accept Him as the Lord and Savior of your heart, you will live forever too.

I would like to thank those treasured deeply in my heart. To my strong and beautiful mother Rose; my kind, courageous, protecting father Breion; my butterfly Brea; my fearless, faithful lioness Khaliyah; my wise stepmama Freda; my successful stepfather Chris; and my joy-filled half brothers Trusten, CJ, and Kallen. The peacemaker, Auntie Ness; the joy carrier, Uncle Deon; the adventurer, Grandma Violet; the merciful; Lola Elsie; my joyful worshiper, Grandma Yvonne. My warrior Grandpa Stanley and my brave Uncle Abrian, and Michael Medlock. I wish I could list you all but you are as numerous as the stars and sand; I love you all.

And now to my beautiful brothers and sisters. Erin, the gentle and fearless; Tsehainish, the light in the darkness; Alexis, the wise and the gentle; Apostle Brian, a true brother and lover of Jesus; Anja, a beautiful rose; Jordyn, a river of grace and mercy; Isabelle, a daughter and a fire that will never go out; Faith, a daughter and God's secret weapon; and last but not least, Skyler, my warrior and beloved. Thank you for all your prayers and encouragement to live and create. God bless you all. These poems are for you and everyone around the world.

TABLE OF CONTENTS

1. Your Hair Is His Glory.........3
United Nations: Mixed/Curly Hair.........4
Royal African Roots: Natural Hair.........6
Silk: Straight Hair.........8
Golden Rays: Blonde Hair.........9
Fire on my Altar: Red Hair.........10
Earth: Brown Hair.........11

2. Your Body Is My Temple.........13
Dovelike: Eyes/Eyelashes.........14
Pure of: Heart.........15
Rivers Flow from Your: Belly.........16
Prepared for Battle: Hands.........17
Gospel of Peace: Feet.........19

3. You Are My Humanity.........21
Inner Man: Men.........22
Virtuous: Woman.........23
I Made You My: Child.........25
There Is Only One: Family.........27

4. Damaged Bodies: The Fallen.........29
    Caged Dove: Mental Trauma.........30
    Wounds: Physical Pain.........31
    Rolling Waves: Emotional Turmoil.........33
    Chains: Spiritual Bondage.........34
    I Am Your Freedom: Deliverance Job.........35

5. You Are My Bride.........37
    Redeemed.........38
    Reborn.........39
    Revival.........40

About the Author.........45

LILIES OF THE VALLEY

An Array of Poems for Humanity Inspired by the Sacred Scriptures of the Bible

She
1 I am a rose of Sharon, a lily of the valleys.
He
2 As a lily among brambles, so is my love among the young women.
She
3 As an apple tree among the trees of the forest, so is my beloved among the young men. With great delight I sat in his shadow, and his fruit was sweet to my taste.
Song of Solomon 2:1-3

1. Your Hair Is His Glory

United Nations: Mixed/Curly Hair.........4
Royal African Roots: Natural Hair.........6
Silk: Straight Hair.........8
Golden Rays: Blonde Hair.........9
Fire on My Altar: Red Hair.........10
Earth: Brown Hair.........11

UNITED NATIONS: MIXED HAIR/ CURLY

Twist. knot. Corkscrew
Black, brown, blond spirals anew.
Wild tamed mane with everywhere to go up.
Spray. pat. mist. fall. waterfall down your back.
Smooth. snap. windbreak through these slides of glory
into soft matted China ink,
turned soft Once kissed by the warmth of the Son.

Swing your glory in the air with praise.
Use your glory to wipe tears away.
Smooth your glory in oil across the feet of your Savior.
Crying out holy holy holy.
I Love your glory says the King of Glory.
The glory in your spirals the world acknowledges
as "boundary."
Boundaries needing straightline order and discipline.
Your glory is choked by the world's hate, curses of every seed
in you since Adam and Eve. Evil tries to curse you as you
reach to Me in your need.
"Straighten your glory, press it away. I don't want to see
your African ancestors,
I don't want to see your Native American braids,
Cut it!
I don't want to see your Asian lengthens,
I don't want to see your Hispanic volume,
tame it.
control it..."
No.
A shouting Voice from Heaven
No!
Don't agree with something I never contemplated.
I desire you to be integrated,
Not agreeing with what the world separated.

1. Your Hair Is His Glory

So Break out of the cages of steaming iron-plated hate.
For this glory rebels against the ways of evil's eyes. Dilated.
Leap in joy of rain from heaven, slides of glory Elevated.
Be free.
Spirals spins and twist.
Be wild.
Curly Glory,
singing freely
never quit.

Royal African Roots: Natural Hair

My treasure in the field.
My crown of Jewels.
Oh how the world does not understand your beauty
Oh how the world does not understand your glory.
Crowned from the roots of your temples.
Your temples are my temples.
Oh when your Anointed oils flow to my altar
from your temples.
Oh Your refined minds are a fragrance to Me.
I love when you just let your glory Be.
Oh Your Natural Glory so sweet,
A fragrance of southern peaches,
Stacked like honeybee hives,
Like palm baskets in perfect balance,
Your glory arises from all your tribes,
Your praises rises and My angels glean,
Your praises move Me to heal
And thus I lean
Closer. Closer. Closer.
For though the world held you in bonds
Although it held you with pain
To burn away your glory in shame
And told you, your Glory was not worthy to be displayed!
I Break Every chain!
For you are mine, I give you My name!
Let Loose your Glory and boast of me! I proclaim!
When your edges grow out at night, my Nazarite, You display
the Royal roots of Africa, the birthplace of the Nations!
Oh My Africa!
Your glory's limits are untamed,
in evil's face you stand unphased for
I, God, gave Your Glory a New Name.
Your Glory is compacted like my touch

1. Your Hair Is His Glory

Only My Purest nature nourishes Your lush
Royal roots.
You're the crown jewels of my heart's pursuits
Founded on the Rock, My African Roots
Hearty, Thick, Rich Abundant Roots
That have no flaws in My Sight,
So never change what I made to Mirror My Marvelous Light
Every knot, every row, every puff, every thing is right
You look just like Your Daddy, crowned with Glory
and endless Might.

Silk: Straight Hair

My hands touch the rippling colors of your silky strands
Come away with me from All life's demands
Lay your Glory down to Me again,
I come to Baptize all this land,
Then to sprout the flowers in the morning in your open hands,
Flashes of Ember, Charcoal, Ruby, Clay, and Gold
Bow down to me day and night, young and old
You lay your Glory down, my finest silk in all the land
You keep coming and you shall be washed in the River
time and time again.
Rise in the morning my silk-stranded Nazarites
Lay down at my altar weeping through the nights
For your beauty is not plain
For your beauty is everything but mundane
I run my fingers through your water-baptized mane
For the deeds of your oil-soaked glory will be proclaimed
Until the end of time
How you washed my feet where I was not welcomed as Adoni
You are beautiful oh my bride
And no one will compare
to the silk strands that you bare.

1. Your Hair Is His Glory

GOLDEN RAYS: BLOND HAIR

Golden beams of light.
Stream lines of glistening topaz Ignite
My heart as I watch your glory glisten in My Glory.
Amber running down the trunk of your neck
Like honeybees from there trees.
Like sweet oil that flows down Aaron's face.
You are my joy,
And display this to the human race.
Lion's mane
My sunflowers,
My waves of grain.
Bursts of light,
My braided swings of joy.
Like the streets of heaven,
You are My delight,
You are wise and you shine brightly among the Nations.
Swing your glory in My Glory .
Shake your treasured strands to the heavens,
Honor God with each ray of gold gifted to your head.
For Joy springs up joy!
So let your Light shine for all to see.
from Stars upon shooting stars.
sparkles of gold glitter gleaming.
Oh your glory shines.
So Shine
shimmering souls shine.

Fire on My Altar: Red Hair

Fire.
flame.
sizzle.
pop.
colors of rose.
Spices of saffron.
Adorn your flaming strands
Shout! "It's His Fire"
Oh your glory is like my eternal flames
Of My Love stirring. concurring,
Oh how your glory shouts, "Let there be Light."
You are a Burning bush
through the trials of rain.
The Crimson bold coals of My delight.
May the fire on your altar never burn out.
Spark the revelation.
The revolution.
You revival strands of fire.
Confident are you My streams of roses
Swing your glory with all its weight.
My Tongues of fire,
My passionate desire of My love are echoed in your strands.
Green vines of olives and healing
surrounded in marvelous colors galore.
Magnificent fired speckles surround your brown,
blue, hazel, green eyes.
How beautiful your strands
My strawberry fields of glory.
How beautiful your strands.

1. Your Hair Is His Glory

Earth: Brown Hair

Dark night skies,
fog in the summer,
olive hues and brown lines of cedar.
Earth.
Oh deepest earth clay reminding us brown hair of our beginnings.
Boats to sail the seas.
Baskets weaved of vines intertwined.
Colors of the Savior's mane.
Oh Israel oh Africa oh Americas. Oh Asias.
My beautiful.
My joys deep pine wood, cinnamon powder pigments.
Your strands are sweet incense to my eyes.
My earthy children.
Chocolates of assorted glory.
Speckles of jelly beans.
Oh aromas of spices.
You are beautiful to my senses.
How sweet are thou aroma,
when your hair sweeps across my feet.
Beautiful.
you are.
Beautiful is what you are.
You are everything to me.
You lack nothing.
My brown-haired lovelies.
You strong cedars.
You are mine.
My beautiful children from the earth.

2. Your Body Is My Temple

Dovelike: Eyes/Eyelashes.........14
Pure of: Heart.........15
River Flow from Your: Belly.........16
Prepared for Battle: Hands.........17
Gospel of Peace: Feet.........19

Dovelike: Eyes/Eyelashes

Black, blond, red. Lashes. lashes.
Feathers of protection,
Wings of butterfly kisses
Paintbrushes of sweet tears
An incense poured out on My feet.
How beautiful.
You will Be known for what you have done through out all the earth My daughter, My son.
Flutter your lashes no longer in the way of idols and loves that can no longer.
Flirt no more with broken cisterns that can never Fill the tomb that I closed forever for your soul to be delivered from.
Look to Me.
I will define your eyes with My love.
Let your lashes not be blacked by this world's façade!
Lashes are what I took on My back for your lashes to be soaked in incense of connection
Incense of healing on your lashes.
Until I come and wipe all
The tears away.
Amen.

2. Your Body Is My Temple

Pure of: Heart

Pitta Patta, Pitta Patta
You move the flow of life through my veins.
You move the flow of my motions all the same.
The flow cannot be interrupted even if I flatline.
The flow cannot be interrupted.
Unless I let these named enemies through my gates:
Depression stops the flow.
Envy stops the flow.
Jealousy stops the flow
Wrath stops the flow
Sin stops the flow.
Death stops the flow.
These beings blacken my crimson engine like volcanic lava touching the sea.
Hardening as newfound land of darkness in my once-ablaze chest cavity.
Pitta Patta, Pitta Patta
His Joy springs the flow.
His Laughter glows the flow
His love moves the flow of life coursing, coursing, sprinting, sprinting through our veins!
Alive.
Alive again pure hands and a clean heart!
I will remove your heart of stone and give you a heart of flesh God.
Heart roaring like a lion
angels soaring
breastplate of righteousness tightened fast, ready for battle!
Pitta Patta, pitta Patta.
Nothing can separate
His love from my soul.
Nothing can separate my heart from This God I Know.

RIVERS FLOW FROM YOUR: BELLY

Floodgates opened wide
No longer trapped inside
Springing forth singing
I'm alive! I'm alive! and I will never die!
When evil tries to come and clog the wells inside
Sing! Oh sing! To your Savior again and again
Until the shadows can't stand
'Cause you're alive!
You're Alive.
From the river flowing from the inside.
You're alive! You're alive.
From The River flowing inside.
The fountain that will never run dry.
Jesus Christ. Jesus Christ.

2. Your Body Is My Temple

Prepared for Battle: Hands

Pure hands and a clean heart.
Pure hands.
Pure hands.
Milk and honey drip drop from heaven,
Run through fingers sticky and sweet,
Smooth and clean.
White as snow.
Crimson red washed white as snow between every aged creases of work.
Hands to work mend,
Bind,
Break.
Healing hands to work.
Spaces separate the days in the week.
We must rest in Him between the work.
Left Hand.
David finger Monday,
Covenant finger Tuesday
Center finger Wednesday
Leading finger Thursday
Approval thumb Friday.
5 days of solid work.
Right Hand.
Approval Monday,
Leading finger Tuesday,
Center finger Wednesday.
Covenant finger Thursday
David finger Friday.
Space to spread out,
Still the work remains
Rest.
Oh hands rest
Oh hands weary from good work.

Lift them to Me.
Calloused.
matured.
muscled.
skilled for Battle
Come Rest In Me.

Gospel of Peace: Feet

My brass drums,
Rhythm keepers,
Forerunners,
Fire starters, movements of life.
Foundations Towers of Lebanon.
Grounded in the streams flowing from the tree of life.
Musical.
Beautiful.
Sacred workers of peace.
Oh Feet the humbler of the proud.
Lowest point of surrender.
Bringer of submission.
Oh feet reminder of where we come from, oh feet.
Oh feet may we look and admire you more often.
Remind us.
Connect us to original beginnings
Oh feet.
Humblers of the human.
Oh feet Remind us God made us from the ground.
Thank you God for my feet. In Jesus' name. Amen.

3. YOU ARE MY HUMANITY

Inner Man: Men………22
Virtuous: Woman………23
I Made You My: Child………25
There Is Only One: Family………27

Inner Man: Men

Hallow Cistern waiting,
Beautiful clay jar swaying,
Waiting for me to hold you still.
Waiting to be poured in,
Your hallow hunger in tunes my ears.
Your groans a beautiful symphony.
More beautiful then my heavenly choirs.
Your deep cries out to my deep.
How well I know it.
Open your mouth so I may fill it.
Breathe in My Spirit,
For you were made to be filled by Me.
Lift up your heads oh ye gates!
Lift up your gates you ancient doors so
the King of Glory can come in.
Who is this King of Glory?
It is I.
The Lord strong and Mighty.
The Lord Mighty in battle.
You my Beloved Adam.
How you hid from Me,
But I never hid from you.
Fourteen generations.
No one can take you from Me,
For I have bought you with a price,
Sealed forever with the Blood of Jesus Christ.
My Eternal Covenant here forever.
My hallow cistern waiting,
Beautiful clay jar swaying,
Waiting for Me to hold you still.
Open your mouth so I may fill it.
Breath My Spirit in so I can seal it.

3. You Are My Humanity

Virtuous: Woman

Oh woman of Faith. How does your Beloved
measure one's worth?
Far above the price of rubies.
Oh woman of nobility.
How Your Husband trusts in you,
Oh woman.
A gatekeeper of the heart.
Your Husband faithfully trusts in you,
Oh gatekeeper of the heart.
She does him good not evil all the days of her life.
You look for work for you are not lazy
You bear food in your arms from the far mountains
for our Family,
Rising before the dawn to feed our Family.
Oh woman of faith how you meditate on all
you do with wisdom.
Oh how you clothed yourself with strength.
Oh how you know what you have purchased is good
And your flame will never go out.
Your hands busily work and stretch to those in need
Oh woman of faith you are fearless.
And you cover all those around you.
You make the clothing of your love for others of wealthy cloth.
The clothing is of strength and honor.
You make your husband proud.
Wisdom seeps from the corners of your lips as
you smile with radiant joy
Kindness is your breath.
You touch not which is forbidden
You eat not of what causes you to die.
Your babies bless you and your husband again every day
Oh woman of virtue you are excellent.

Your inner beauty will never fade and
you shall be praised in the gates of heaven.
Give her the fruit of her labor Lord.
Bless the Virtuous woman of Faith.

3. You Are My Humanity

I Made You My: Child

I know you.
Little one,
Unknown to the world.
Nameless heartbeat
I know you.
I know your name.
I knew you before the beginning of time.
You cling to your mother inside the womb.
I was the one that formed the bond to cling you,
For you shall cling to your father and mother all the days of
your lives until you find another to cling to,
called your
Wife. Called your,
Husband.
I have Perfectly formed the covenant of marriage
3 into 1
Not 2 into 2
Or 1 into 1
But 3 into 1
A love covenant so strong when you're one together I create
life.
Oh baby. You are not a mistake.
You are my arrow.
Oh mother let Me help you in every way.
You are a birther of Life
Oh father stop all the hate of yourself.
You are the coverer of Life
To create a child. You must love yourself and love her as Christ
loved the church and died for her.
Hurt you have no portion in our bodies
Shame you have no portion in our children
Accuser if you have forced yourself in Jesus will force you out.
Jesus heal our family

Jesus heal our mothers
Jesus heal our fathers
Jesus heal our land.
Amen.

THERE IS ONLY ONE: FAMILY

I am the Vine.
and You are Mine.
Ecclesia,
Can you not see,
When you bow,
And sing Alleluias to Me,
you bind Your branches to Mine.
Now it is time to combine,
And Let the fragrance Arise.
For there is only one family,
And in My love you are tied,
I The Son, You the Heirs
God our Father who knows all the hairs,
On your Head and not the Tail.
The Alpha and Omega will never fail,
Our Father never lets the gates of Hell prevail,
And when the Son of Man who tore the veil,
Descends again to send the devil to hell,
This Family will shout All Hail! All Hail!
Our Father God and King Jesus All Hail!
This Family will live forever to tell the tale,
Of How King Jesus Destroyed all evil!

4. Damaged Bodies: The Fallen

Caged Dove: Mental Trauma.........30
Wounds: Physical Pain.........31
Rolling Waves: Emotional Turmoil.........33
Chains: Spiritual Bondage.........34
I Am Your Freedom: Deliverance Job.........35

Caged Dove: Mental Trauma

Just a quiet soul in this crazy world,
Lost and you're afraid to even speak a sound.
Your gentle soul afraid to even say your own name,
For you fear how they see you are alone.
When you try and strive,
You're knocked down to your feet,
You stand back up tall but the whispers strike you
down to your knees
"She thinks that she is strong," they laugh in your ear.
But they lie eternally for you are more then what you appear.
Like a thief in the night He has paid the price for your life
And you stop and realize that the curses can't
pierce you like knives
They have no authority to take your life
So you open your mouth and sing to break the fright
Because the demons cannot have your mind
For you are given the power to live from the Son
So rise, to your freedom, from your mistakes, from your past
From your slavery oh to yourself. Fly you caged dove fly.

Wounds: Physical Pain

Dark bloodied open,
Bruised eyes, broken
Lay down so I can heal them
Scab infected love ejected
Let me pour My love over you.
Bath in My milk and oil
Let Me pour my medicine on you
Soak in My presence
Soak in My Word
Soak in My perfume
Oh beloved wallowing in your blood
I picked you up and washed you cleaned
I nursed you to health with a harvest you did not glean.
All that I have is given to you.
My tree's leaves are yours to heal all the Nations
Come.
Drink of Me.
Learn of Me.
For I know you cannot stand
But I won't put too much on you that you can't bear
For I know what you are missing
I won't let you bear it alone.
For I know what they took away
My love is your medicine.
For every broken heart
My love stitches you up and keeps treating you.
Until all that is left is a scar
Glorify Me with your scar
Your scar is a broken chain above your head.
Oh sing of how it is broken.

Oh sing how I healed you My beloved.
For I love your songs of praise.
For I love to heal you oh My Nations.
My bride. My love. My bride. My love. My bride.

4. Damaged Bodies: The Fallen

ROLLING WAVES: EMOTIONAL TURMOIL

Roaring, crash, dripping, crash
Roll. Roll. Roll. Undertow
Rage. Confusion. Impulsion. Condemnation
Roaring, Crash, Dripping, crash
Roll. Roll. Roll. Under....
Peace...
Roll...
Be Still...
Rage. Break! Confus....
Peace My Child
I am Here
I am near the waves are split for you
Walk My child.
One foot up... one skip...one run
Jesus!
The winds and Waves know Your name. Now I can run to You!
Oh Jesus! My toil is over. My winds have changed!
Hallelujah!

CHAINS: SPIRITUAL BONDAGE

Chains come with many names,
Chains weigh to make you lame
To keep you from laments
The groans trapped in boxes inside
You were never meant to hide
But the demons hover over your treasure at night
Binding your sin around it in chains. Chains. Chains
Choking you to remain the same. Same. Same
Until you choke in shame.
Unnamed you remain in the chains.
They are deceiving as they're covered in the idol gold
They are deceiving until you see your heart's grown stone cold
From rebellion, sickness, disease, lies, rage
The list piles and piles and piles
But I hear the chains falling.
I hear them shattering
I see them breaking off!
Hallelujah!
Jesus!
You are here!
When Darkness thought I could not hear,
You came to break every chain!
Bursting Your Glory!
You ripped the chains off my back. Off my eyes off my legs!
You are afraid of no sin!
You stab the demons
You grind the chains into dust.
So I arise!
I arise and shout Jesus!
I am freed Indeed!
Oh Lord Thank You!
You have heard my plea!

4. Damaged Bodies: The Fallen

I Am Your Freedom: Deliverance Job

Wandering soul to whom do you belong?
Truth What is Truth?
The Way
What is the Way?
Life What is Life?
Wandering souls how hungry are you all.
You toss day and night and have not Light,
Your stomach scratches and begs
until He comes with His Word that beckons

I Am. I Am The Way, The Truth, The Life.

Peels of Thunder erupting with millions of angels,
As your tears sop the floor
Visions of The Father on His throne
As you reach your hands up for more.
You're all and everything I have longed for
You scream in Joy
As He asks for your life
You remember all your Strife
And He covers it all with His stripes.
For today is a new day.
And with a heart cry you shout okay!
For He is everything you've hungered for so don't delay.
Lay your sins on the altar and watch the Son burn them away
For you have become a Son, you have become
a daughter on this New Day.

5. You Are My Bride

Redeemed.........38
Reborn.........39
Revival.........40

Redeemed

Redeemed with Holy Tears,
Redeemed with a slap on His face,
Redeemed with the ripping out of His beard,
Redeemed when they spat on His Face.
Redeemed when they mocked His Authority,
Redeemed when they stripped Him Bare,
Redeemed when they torn His Flesh to bone,
Redeemed when they drug Him back to the cellar,
Redeemed when they forced the crown into His skull
Redeemed when they Shouted crucify Him
Redeemed when He chose Barnabas' death
Redeemed when He carried the cross with Simon
Redeemed When He laid His body down
Redeemed when He let them pierce His Hands
Redeemed when He let them pierce His Feet
Redeemed when He gasped for air three days
Redeemed When His blood ran on the ground like Abel's
Redeemed When He committed His Spirit to His Father
Redeemed When He ripped the veil
Redeemed when He shook the Earth
Redeemed when the temple fell
Redeemed when they looked on the One whom They Pierced
Redeemed when His bones weren't broken
Redeemed when His body lay in Joseph's Tomb
Redeemed When He rose From hell after Three Days!
Redeemed When He had the keys of death
and hades in His Hand
Redeemed When He set His Spirit on All the land
I am Redeemed because King Jesus sits at God's Right Hand.

5. You Are My Bride

REBORN

Reborn In the Fire of His Burning Love
By Mercy gifted only from above,
There is no Grace in all the earth like this,
There is no sin in this world I would ever miss.
I'm in love with The Sacrifice You made for our Hearts,
To be born again In Your presence no longer apart.
searching for our Father in our works has ceased,
For we could never earn Your Spirit and Eternal Peace.
So I can only bring my brokenness.
I lay myself down in all my mess.
To be reborn, Jesus in Who You Are.
I have absolutely no worries about tomorrow.
For until You resurrect our bodies and this world
from the dark.
Here We stand, Ours Lights Ignited By your Spark.
Salt to the earth,
You draw all to Rebirth.
Redeemed by the Lamb,
We will sing to all the lands.
Renewed when we sing of Your love again
and again and again.
For He is the One who Was, And Is and Is to come forever and
Refreshed for our lives have been raised from the dead.
For He Is the Only One Who could pay our debt.
So reach out now He's waiting for you,
For all that you have been told is Spirit and Truth.

REVIVAL

You are evidence of the Rebirth
So go forth in all the earth
Revive the dead bodies
Revive the dead dreams
Revive yourself at My feet
There is no way you can do this with out Me
I the Lord have called you to awaken
Not just yourselves but whole cities
So go forth in all the earth and make disciples
for My Kingdom
For your treasures in Heaven are better then
the earth's so leave them.
For your love is My delight
To love them is to invite them Into My Marvelous Light
Be Strong.
Be courageous.
Be brave.
For I will never leave you nor forsake you in all My Ways.

SCRIPTURES FOR EACH SECTION OF POEMS

1. Your Hair Is His Glory
Numbers 6:5, Song of Solomon, 1 Corinthians 11:3-16, Ephesians 4:23-24

2. Your Body Is My Temple
Song of Solomon 1:15
Psalm 24:4
John 7:37- 38
Psalm 144:1
Ephesians 6:15

3. You Are My Humanity
Genesis 2:6
Proverbs 31
Psalm 139
Genesis 2, John 15, Acts 2:42-47, Romans 11:11.

4. Damaged Bodies: The Fallen
1 Peter 5:8

Leviticus 14, Mark 1:40-45
Matthew 8:23-27, Luke 8:22-25
Matthew 8:28-34
Psalm 32:7, Psalm 34, Galatians 5:1, James 4:7, 1 John 4:4.

5. You Are My Bride
Isaiah 43:1, Romans 5:3, Galatians 3:23-25, Hebrews 9:22
John 3, John 14:6
Revelation

Overall:
Matthew 26:6-13, Jesus anointed by the weeping woman

Thank you for reading my first poetic creation, *Lilies of the Valley*. Be blessed forever and ever until our Lord Jesus comes again.

Love,
LaAsia J. Medlock

ABOUT THE AUTHOR

*L*ilies of the Valley is an assortment of poems that was created for the Bride of Christ, the Church, and all those who would answer the invitation into God's family.

LaAsia J. Medlock was born in Aiken, South Carolina, but raised in Galena, Ohio. She is a daughter, worshiper, and creator. As a member of Hope City House of Prayer in Columbus, Ohio, and a student at The Ohio State University, LaAsia added debut author to her growing list of accomplishments with this book.

www.ingramcontent.com/pod-product-compliance
Lightning Source LLC
Chambersburg PA
CBHW071648040426
42452CB00009B/1799